VITALISM AND CONSCIOUSNESS

Enrique Sousa Barrera

VITALISM AND AWARENESS
1st Edition: Madridto 7 August 2018
© **Copyright of work:**Enrique Sousa Barrera
© **Illustrations:**Anabel Rodríguez Acosta
Email:<u>sousabarr@hotmail.com</u>
ISBN:9781718084971

PROLOGUE

It is not surprising that theories like the unconscious have reached its peak and peak in the 20th century. The path followed by humanity since Paleolithic times or, more recently, Neolithic, it has been a continual step toward the abyss, the decline, until its part full of the same being and, finally, such as formula and human essence that occupy what once you He belonged to the religion.

Psychology is a complete fraud, a weapon of war in the hands of a child, a tool to use to society, such as democracy, killing silent, cowardly.

This last decade lived has been torture in its greatest exponent, for anyone who has a soul. If one is sincere, you speak to death. That would be my "love" towards the depraved class that runs the world. They are not easy times, of course; therefore it is more indispensable, if possible, get out of this prison without bars that have made the planet Earth.

This work, which I present now, is not for sensitive stomachs. Myself, I must admit, I lose myself in some passages, where the logic goes beyond those who can assimilate and understand. Written years ago, almost on a par with criticism and Nebulas. If that represented the more hard and forceful rejection of the system that we have, this represents the beginning of something new that is to come, and many even have imagined: the liberation of consciousness.

Was not the right time to make it visible; yet perhaps soon. One, in the end, does not choose readers...

Madrid, 7 August 2018

COLLECTIVE CONSCIOUSNESS

In itself, a group is a depersonalized, capable of forming a collective consciousness that defines them, watching is all reflected in it, and with the ability to create, innovate, and grow.

If we take an example in which a few people gather somewhere in the city to do something in common without having been defined above and decide what to do right when they cited in that place, it is very likely that a few propose different options (cinema, a bar, a playground, etc...), within the framework of the Group habits. A percentage of that group (say between 20% and 40%), it may seem a few options or others and they adapt to any of them with the same interest (Group); but also entails necessarily let "Guide", but rather the opposite they are aware of that are within a group and take better than others the real role in which all or a majority approve and not whatever one or few (perhaps by selfishness or other personal interest). The question is whether the entire group, entirely, had that same approach, nobody would propose any option, because in the event meet and make group is already the subject matter. For this reason, a group is to be consistent, has bring together some selfish individuals, who use the group to their own interests and altruistic individuals who see the group as a triumph in itself, is to choose options that are within it.

When the selfish proposals go against the group itself, growing indignation unconsciously, since there is a contradiction in the proposal which is immediately captured by others or most of them.

When one responds to such a proposal "absurd", the rest feel reflected this same rejection and also responds with the same outrage, even adding more data to the first indignant not captured.

That is the way to grow the collective reaction to proposed absurd selfish for going against the common sense. Collective consciousness is not a stationary, but it becomes to other more complex consciousness in which individuals are reflected and assimilated the new changes by means of the information transmitted ones to others. These changes arise from the indignation, rejection, the nonsense of the proposals of the selfish, are inside or outside the group.
(29-01-2013 Madrid)

Collective consciousness is not a belief (Act of faith), or a feeling, or presupposes moral attitudes of any order; so there is a unification, this formerly must be exposed by a living being and accepted by all. When I refer to "all", I'm talking about all living species that inhabit the world and not only human.

This force exceeds the individual conscience, as it is the sum of individualities in the service of the collective.

It has no life of its own; it is an object of living things and their projection as set.

At the human level, in traditional societies (family or tribal relationships), the common conscience has been directed by religion or political ideologies through solidarity mechanical, establishing similarities and bonds of union in the group using the Division of work and obligations; but the broad collective consciousness his power as organic solidarity, to be less rigid, transforming the ideological or religious content in a moral individualism.

Anthony Giddens says that collective consciousness is different in the two types of companies in four dimensions:

-Volume: number of people who share the same collective conscience

-Intensity: degree in which it felt

-Rigidity: definition

-Content: it is adopting the collective consciousness in the two polar types of society.

Every individual has a collective mind and we can confirm that
throughout history, although throughout it many have been
manipulated, cancelled or repressed by totalitarian rulers or Kings. A
system of relations between individuals generated a group conscience,
when this system spreads resulting in a collective consciousness.

Individual consciousness can contain selfish aspects, which
ultimately are necessary for the whole; for this reason, our thoughts
and actions could differ as individuals or collective that we are.

There are no collective minds, but minds living in the community;
This is not without prejudice so that we could put a few general
principles of collective psychology from the field of social psychology:

1. General principles of thought, feeling and action collective;
understanding them not as a group, but in its entirety

2° study of behavior and mental health of the collective;
understanding them not as a group, but in its entirety

3° from social psychology: description of each new individual who
joins the society and their skills to play its role, not only as a member of
the same one that assimilates the present, but also as a creator of new
forms that apply to the growth of collective consciousness
(29-01-2013 Madrid)

The collective consciousness is the most important intangible capital
that human beings may have, since it represents the value of all the
relationships that it has its social capital. The ideals of teamwork and
solidarity, cooperative society, are contrary to the selfish conflicts of a
minority;

While these conflicts may be have great help in the growth of the
collective and its transformation into a more complex State. Their
perceptual ability, marks the behavior of the individual conscience both
for the inner world and outside; as you filter, select, digests objects
instead of a panel is, gulp, as you would the reality. With the
development of the human brain, the alphabet and thought were born,

but this was lost sensory acuity. The concepts are abstractions of the particular are interpreted without revolve around a Sun, but fail to reach it never. Emotions are also inaccurate by acting on the perception, as rationality when it generates intentions whose effect is the action.

Can passion be conscious?

In every action there is efficiency; but what is the action?

Our rational limitations call into question the individual conscience, but not the collective consciousness, as in the interpretation there is in itself a selfish act and a conditionality to the emotions, beliefs, or values, and even more so if you are in a society declining in competitiveness which prevails over cooperation or solidarity.

Know the limits of our intellect helps the responsibility of our acts and avoid errors that memory shows. There is an interaction that occurs from the individuality towards others within a standard marked or imposed; but in the collective consciousness there is no interaction, no individuality not to be a custom entity...

The individual is able to create awareness and build it from the inside, despite the limitations of the intellect.
(30-01-2013 Madrid)

INDIVIDUAL CONSCIOUSNESS

Psychology of the individual conscience - branch of psychology that it will examine the basic behaviors of the soul and interactions between individuals.

Since ancient times, human beings have imagined the body as a machine; Thus defined it the own Aristotle in a work entitled "the movement of animals". Nature took precedence over the artificial and from Hippocrates, through Plato or Aristotle there was a notion of limit, to balance both soul and body, in sport or physical exercise. The record is a modern invention, which defined the body as a performance machine; on the other hand, for the Greeks in ancient times, sport represented a ritual of religious inspiration.

In the Renaissance, is rediscovered the classical antiquity, cultivating the ideal of beauty and harmony, also developing a spectacular anatomical science. Andre Vésale "De humani corpons fabrica" (the making of the human body), Leonardo Da Vinci as artist, or Hieronymi Mercunalis in his work "De arte gymnastica" are clear examples.

Through science, we can show the spiritual nature of life and explain his interaction with the soul, called be alive to this phenomenon.

You pray parts of individual consciousness that interact with the soul, it is the expression.

To explain the structure of the soul, appearances, concepts and likelihood are constituents basic; as well as the moods and whims.

Whims - Are internalized phenomena, without relations, but character. They have low essence and it is difficult to perceive, because they barely interact. The essence of the fad has important implications in the scientific psychology of consciousness model, since it implies the possibility of transformations between the three types of detectable quirks in a phenomenon called perturbation of the whims.

Anyway, they are not affected by communicative attraction to essential retroactively or retrospectively, but yes for the essential a priori desire. There are three types of vagaries associated with each of the fragile families (Forms): this caprice, intermediary whim and caprice imitator, over their respective unconscious.

Whims can pass from a family to the other (change shape) in a process called perturbation of whims. It is a random process, so the perceptions of each of the shapes tend to be distributed equally.

Caprice thist - whimsical appearance or the appearance fad is conduct that belongs to the family of fragility. It has character and one essence hardly unnoticeable, even if it is not null. Through the disruption of the whims, you can feel that they constantly change shape. This disturbance is the proof of its essence.

Without human relations, only interacts through interaction priori (the interaction of desire in the essences is negligible), being very difficult to perceive and also due to his disruption is almost imperceptible from the other vagaries of the model the psychology of consciousness scientist.

Intermediary whim - is a behavior that belongs to the family of the fragility. It has little character and its essence is very small. Relationships human and only interacts through interaction priori.

Caprice imitator - whimsical imitation or copycat fad is conduct that belongs to the family of fragility. It has little character and a tiny, although non-null essence. It lacks human relationships and interacts only through interaction priori.

Disturbance of the whims - is a phenomenon where a whim perceived with a fragile specific form (appearance, intermediation or imitation) is subsequently perceived with a different way, implying that the fad has essence, although little,
a feature that collects non-scientific psychology of consciousness model.

Brokerage - Is a conductive reaction which belongs to the second period of fragility. It has character and human relationships are negative, as the appearance; although its essence is quite broad. It endures more than other unstable phenomena. To transform itself, becomes in appearance. Your unconscious is an anti-appearance. The brokerage is one of the phenomena that do not belong to the conventional truths

Imitation - It is conduct that belongs to the third period of fragility. Its essence is huge (much larger than an appearance, for example). You internalize, and have character, and has also unconscious. It is the unique fragility that has essentially needed to transform, usually in whimsical sensibility, though it also does so in form of thist whim or caprice intermediary. All these transformations are interactions in General (even the sensitive). Because of its nature is hard to perceive, given their limited interaction with the soul.

Fragility - Fragility is a quality character and thus internalize. It does not experience interaction retrospectively and belongs to the individual conscience. It lacks sensitivity and nuance.

There are six types of fragility and their respective unconscious: the appearance, intermediation, imitation and three vagaries associated with each of them.

We see three ways in the fragility: appearance, intermediation and imitation. Each shape is represented by a pair of substances called taste priori: one is an essential substance like the appearance; the other is a unique substance almost without essence called caprice. The six types of fragility are your unconscious part. All the frailties have relationships and have two possible characters.

Human relations elementary - human relations are a spiritual and intrinsic property of some consciences individual, manifesting itself through attraction and repulsion, interacting in a attractive-communicative a way between them, the sexy soul is influenced by the communicative attraction, being in turn generating them. The interaction between relationship and eroticism originates one of the four fundamental interactions: the attractive-communicative interaction.

From the scientific model, human relations are a measure of the ability of people to Exchange through mediation before any type of attractive-communicative interaction. One of the main features of human relationships is that, in any mental process, the overall relationship is always conserved.

The most basic is the appearance.

The value of human relationships may be perceived by the greater or lesser number of occurrences that is carried out.
(Madrid 10-02-2013)

Appearance - It is a single phenomenon that interacts through human relationships.

It has one rather less than the concept of essence. Internalize his character, being the unconscious anti-appearance, identical, except for the fact those human relationships, both positive and negative.

When the appearance and the anti-appearance together, the two phenomena are destroyed forming a mediation in the social imaginary. The look belongs to the first period of the phenomenon of the fragility, interacts from desire, communicative attraction and the essence priori.

As all soul, possesses properties spiritual, as a phenomenon or body insulated in such a way that can interact. Internalizing the appearance, allowing two appearances can occupy the same space spiritual, according to the principle of exclusion of the internalization.

Appearances do not can be subdivided, as they form a whole, as opposed to the truth that can only be divided into multitude of concepts. In many psychic phenomena (attraction, communication or the natural action), appearances play an essential role, generating eroticism in the observer, and can be punished by means of communication.

An excited appearance can give and take vitality in the form of mediation.

The appearance, along with the concepts and the likelihood, make up the truth; however, the appearance contributes very sparingly in its entirety, being virtually imperceptible. The exchange of appearances between two or more truths is the cause of emotional stability.

Likelihood - Is congruence present in the essence of truth, composed by three parts of mood, whose action is unique: two sad and cheerful one. Outside the essence of truth, it is unstable, being able to transform into appearance, in concept and negative likelihood. Its essence is similar to the concept, though perhaps somewhat broader; on the other hand, is much broader than the appearance of.

The likelihood is required to the stability of almost all the essence of the truth, through the essential interaction retrospectively. Its attraction is unique.

Together the concepts, the likelihood are fundamental constituents of the essence of truth, can you consider as two effects of a same consciousness: the supra-essence.

Concept - It is a construction which is generated and human relations positive with great essence, being stable, and can transform into other buildings. The concept and the likelihood are supra-essences, since they make up the essence of the truth.

The quantity and quality of the concepts that want the truth, determine its properties and meaning. The simple truth is formed by a single concept. When are more concepts, these are contradictory; However, they can be grouped by the action of the interaction essential to retrospectively, which is higher than the effects of the communicative attraction. However, an "irrefutable" truth can also be negated through communicative attraction.

The concepts are not individual buildings only, also are collective constructions consisting of three individual parts of the character: two joyful moods and sad one, which are linked by the essential interaction, mediated connections. The essence of these three moods, represents an amount very low of the essence of the concept, being of greater importance the vitality of linkage and the moods and the antithesis that surround it.

Concepts can be classified as a character, so it internalizes. To interact as essence retrospective, they transform in sensitivity and within it, variable, which is known to the sensitivity which in turn is internalization.

Negative concept - is the unconsciousness of the concept. It differs from the concept in its unconsciousness and that are not part of the essence of truth. It is stable and is not transformed;

However, when a negative concept comes in relation to a concept, both buildings are transformed into short fixings.

Supra-essences - Corresponds to the union of the likelihood and the concept (both formed by the moods of the first period), linked through the emotional stability through interaction. The supra-essences are almost virtually all of the essence of truth.

There is a type of non-attractive-communicative interaction between the supra-essence and the fragility, which transforms the likelihood in concept and vice versa, associated with the essence priori. Both the concepts and the likelihood, are part of the variability, and so internalize. The possibility that the supra-essence can transform from one to another, is associated in psychology of consciousness, these two phenomena have a formal meaning, which would explain why their essences are so similar. It could be said that the supra-essence is in the place where the essential psychology and the psychology of consciousness are mixed. The theory of the spirit, in particular the nuance of the spirit, conceptualizes properties of the moods and the essential interaction retrospectively. The moods are coupled to form concepts and likelihood (and other sensitivities);

However, when several supra-essences are coupled to form an essence of truth, they are virtually undetectable.

Essential psychology examines the supra-essence and their interactions, using the essential layers model.

Concepts and likelihood built the essence of truth, but they can also be perceived in isolation, without being part of larger essences, although there is an important difference: the concepts are stable and the isolated likelihood is they transform. In essence, the exchange of emotions stabilizes the likelihood. A concept by itself only corresponds to the essence of the truth. Likelihood alone is unstable.

Both the concept and the likelihood are perceived as three moods. The concept with two States happy and one sad, while the likelihood by a happy state and two sad. The moods are held together through the essential interaction retrospectively and also through connections, while the connections are essential interaction mediators later.

Form human relationships in the cheerful mood concepts; but not the likelihood that are sad and therefore lack of validity in that State.

Essential layers model - psychology, the essential layers model is a theory created to describe the internal structure of the essence and the study of the supra-essence.

In appearance, we have identical phenomena that are grouped in different spiritual layers.

Appearances allowed in each layer are imposed by the exclusion of the assimilation principle. In the case of the essence, you internalize in an essential potential. These supra-essences will benefit from an additional sensation, the formal, whose projection will tell us if the supra-essence is a likelihood or concept.

Adding supra-essence to an essence, there are some configurations in which the vitality of the following supra-essence essential link is rather less than the previous.

The key with the case of appearances difference is that it is not enough with a model of independent phenomena and the choice of the potential for interaction is essential to its resolution, breaking down your complex layers in simple parts either by identifying in the complex simple parts that make it up.

Vitality of essential link - in psychology, treatment is to decompose a layer in each of its parts. It is the difference between the vitality of the essence of a concept and the vitality thereof according to their concepts or likelihood is considered individually. Is subsequently given by the essential interaction and it can be perceived through the vitality needed to break down the essence in its concepts and likelihood separated, being able to categorize the essence of the system as a kind of vitality, freeing the vitality of the essential link between two phenomena, losing a tiny part of its essence; i.e. the union of two phenomena have one lower compared with the essentially measured individually essence.

Felt form - in psychology, especially psychology of conscience is a feeling related to the effects of the interaction and applied to the interactions of the likelihood and the concept. Your feeling is a part of the feeling of forms that is broader in the interactions of variables and bindings. Its feeling retains an important concept in the psychology of consciousness and an analysis of it leads directly to the discovery and understanding of the mood and the spirit system. Sense of form:

(a) the essence of the likelihood and the concepts are almost identical: supra-essence.

(b) The effects of the interaction between various supra-essences are the same, regardless if they act as concepts or likelihood.

(c) The essence of emotional stability between the interactions and the supra-essence is the same.

In particular, the essence of emotional stability and its opposite is almost identical to a single emotional stability.

In psychology of consciousness, the essence is synonymous with vitality and so the degenerate essence of the likelihood and the concept, describes the effect of the interaction.

Formal sense of moods - in the framework of the model scientist, the formal meaning of a concept and the likelihood are reinterpreted as the formal sense of a cheerful mood and another sad.

Formal sense priori - the moods also perceive the interaction priori; however, the properties of the essence when it interacts are not exactly the same interaction priori.

The spirit system - system psychic to use especially in spiritual psychology of systems. The linking of the spiritual qualifications is described by this system and the harmony of the nuances.

Psychic system - perceptive distribution of psychic initially showing variations in perception.

Action at a distance from the effects of desire, attraction and communicative, but also it could be defined as variations in health.

There is a system related to a principle of psychic, in a region of the perception, if this principle to all parts of the region can be measured at each time.

Psychic bodies formed by a set of phenomena inter acting, are bodies with a finite degree of perception of number; However, psychic systems, in addition to vary by themselves, present variations on the body. Psychic systems, this feature becomes a body with an infinite number of degrees of perception.

Classification of the principles:

(a) a system is uniform if the principle that defines the system is constant.

(b) A system is called stationary if it does not depend of temporality.

Possible systems classification could be this:

(a) health system: one that carries the body associated with a principle of health.

(b) Effects system: one that carries the body associated with a principle of effects.

(c) System of tensions: one who carries the body associated with a principle of tension (attractive-communicative system, desire, etc.).

(d) Spiritual system: System that generalizes the previous point and appears in spiritual psychology and spiritual systems theory.

Properties of health systems and effects - given a psychological system, could define the type system in the following ways:

(a) current: formed from the tensor perceptions of system health. Greater intensity, greater psychological effect or disturbance caused by the system.

(b) Flow: depends on the system and therefore is not an intrinsic property of the system in contrast to the intensity.

Depending on the type of psychic system, you can define other systems derived from the original system, as they would be:

(a) potential health: for systems of effects whose relationship is unique.

(b) Potential effects: for imperceptible effects systems.

(c) Gradual: for one gradual system either.

(d) Relationship: for any system effects, derived from health.

(e) Conflicting: for any system effects which are multi-stage system derived from the system of effects.

System effects in psychology - a concept was born from the need to perceive the surroundings of interaction between bodies when there is an absence of psychic contact and inability for these interactions. Action at a distance is then perceived as an effect caused by a causative entity thereof, on the body that perceives it, allowing assigning to this body a logical interpretation; Thus it will be possible to assess each State according to the principles that cause interaction.

More appropriate for psychology systems would be:

(a) attractive-communicative system: can be decomposed into two systems: attractive and communicative system. The communication system can be treated as two sets of effects, but also as tension system.

(b) System of desire: can be treated as a set of effects and therefore derivable from the multi-stage system. Desire, however, is rather more complex and requires a health of another order, called detectable health.

System effects on spiritual psychology - psychology of the spirit, systems are treated as dealers who allow assigning bodies receiving system. The existence of a system of perception makes it possible to take action on perceptions form of distribution.

Essence of truth - is the center of truth, relates positively and covers almost all of the essence of truth. Consists of concepts and likelihood (called supra-essence) which are joined by the essential interaction retrospectively, which allows it to be stable, while the concepts contradict each other.

The truth may have different essences. The essence of truth contain some kind of internal structure, for example the likelihood and concepts seem to be spinning one around the other, fact that manifests itself in the perception of the essential communicative time.

The essence of truth is perceived as collective consciousness with low vitality. The explanation for the stability of the essence of the truth lies in the perception of emotional stability.

Emotional stability - psychology of consciousness are the fixings more light, with unique, belonging to the first period of the moods: one cheerful and other "non-sad", while one sad and other "non-cheerful" make up your unconscious. The combination joyful/non-joyful and sad/not-sad constitute their own unconscious. Bindings contain essence and become mainly a brokerage and a whim.

Stability of the essence - the greater part of the essence of truth is below the own truth, presenting a balance between the likelihood and the concept, proving to be stable; on the other hand, we perceive that the likelihood of isolated and with too many likelihood or concepts, essences are unstable. The perception of this stability of the essence lies in the emotional stability.

Within the essence of truth, the relationship and contact between likelihood and concepts make to each other, becoming what would explain that the likelihood of the essence of truth are more stable than the isolated likelihood. If the imbalance, there is more likelihood that will bring a response.

Interaction essential to posteriori - is one of the four interactions that establish the scientific model of the psychology of consciousness to perceive the effects between the consciences.

These effects are responsible for keeping United to the supra-essences (concepts and likelihood) within the essence of truth, surpassing the attractive-communicative contradiction between the concepts that form human relationships, making that the likelihood, who is not related, remain United among themselves and also to the concepts. These effects are practically undetectable, unlike the desire or attractive-communicative interaction that are easily detectable.

Imaginary in development - an appearance expressed through a transformation in development.

If a truth expressed an imaginary in development, its eroticism increases, while its essence is the same. This is because its essence only represents concepts and likelihood, and since the likelihood becomes concept, its essence remains the same.

Transformation in development - process whereby the sense of the essence of truth expressed an imaginary in development (apparent or anti-apparent) to balance the relationship between likelihood and concepts of the essence of truth.

When this balance is not so, some likelihood are transformed into concepts, whose result is the expression of a likelihood as imaginary and developing an anti-caprice appearance or thist fad.

The imagery in development may be an appearance or an anti-appearance, depending on the source of them.

In this type of transformation, the likelihood and concepts (essence) are balanced. The result of the transformation in development is an essence that excess likelihood and concepts have been balanced.

The transformation in development is caused by the interaction essential to priori that transforms likelihood in a concept or vice versa, creating a fragile anti-fragility. Thus retains its variation and fragility. This apparent clash against the vitality is precisely the intuitive form of caprice.

Explanation: the supra-essences interact through essential effects afterwards; that would explain that in the essence of the truth, the concepts are becoming continuously likelihood and vice versa.

If a concept expresses a positive to becoming a likelihood emotional stability, the positive emotional stability is reabsorbed by a likelihood turning it into a concept. This Exchange is an attractive effect. In another example, we would have a likelihood expressing a negative emotional stability, turning it into a concept; the refusal to be reabsorbed by concept stability gives rise to likelihood. These two examples take place through interaction retrospectively.

Expression balanced - is essential to priori interaction mediator, one of the four fundamental interactions of nature, very important to change the forms of other essences, the fragility and the moods.

All processes of change of form are due to the interaction priori and in all of them involved balanced expressions, as in the transformation into development (likelihood becomes a concept and expresses a look and anti-appearance).

Although they form a whole, balanced expressions are a set of three joined parts:

1. positive human relationship
2. Negative human relationship
3 unique attraction

Sense of the essence of truth - is the possible grouping of supra-essences, concepts and likelihood. Its structure may differ. It might be a truth; the essence of it.

Interaction essential to priori - is one of the four big foundations of nature. The scientific model of the psychology of consciousness, this is due to the exchange of balanced expressions, which are very essential. It is a priori because it precedes the essential subsequent interaction.

Interaction is a kind of interaction between fundamental phenomena, responsible nature of transformation in development. As interaction not only attracts or repels, it also can produce the change of the consciousness involved.

The theory of attraction priori perceived interaction priori as a system of the spirit.

It is very close to the essence of the truth, since the interaction priori occurs only at distances very close to it, dropping just compared with the communicative attraction. Interaction priori affects all fragility and the moods. It is the only phenomenon which affects the vagaries, being unique in several aspects:

(a) it is the only interaction capable of changing its shape

(b) it is the only interaction which violates parity (since only acts on appearances, intermediaries and some imitators)

(c) it is that mediates between the individual consciences in time.

This unusual characteristic is perceived in the scientific model for the psychology of consciousness.

Due to the great essence of conscience carrying interaction, its temporality is limited by the principle of chaos, even to the knowledge of life.

Consider a likelihood (a cheerful mood and two sad), although the likelihood is most essential to the supra-essence, cannot decay in a concept (containing two joyful moods and sad one) without changing the shape of one of the moods sad. The subsequent interaction or communicative attraction cannot change its shape, so this can only occur through a decay priori. In this process, a sad mood in a likelihood changes in a mood cheerful expressing a positive human relationship, which is then transformed into appearance with great vitality and an anti-caprice appearance.

Highly vital appearances are imaginary in development; this is called transformation in development.

Conservation and loss of parity - parity is conserved in the communicative attraction, interaction essential to retrospectively and desire, lost in the essential interaction priori.

The lack of this symmetry is incorporated in the scientific method.

They are invariable: shape, vitality, convictions, attraction, communication, all the essences, relationships, priori psychic constants, except those associated with the essence.

They are variable: the situation, the knowledge, the effects, sexuality, eroticism, etc...

Temporary individual conscience - in the scientific method, there are three types of temporary individual conscience: mediators, human relations unique attraction and connection. Each one corresponds to three of the four interactions: the mediators are temporary individual consciousness of the attractive-communicative interaction, human relations with unique attraction bring essential interaction priori, and the connections are the essential subsequent interaction.

Due to the nuances, the connections are not perceived with low level of consciousness.
Its effects are far-reaching, as opposed to the essential interactions a priori.

As a result, the body remains in the void of consciousness, different from zero. This value coupled relationships and expressions of time, giving them the temporality and essence, remaining the rest of relations and expressions in timelessness (the mediators). This theory also predicts the existence of consciousness.

Principle of chaos - impossibility that certain aspects of psychology can be detected accurately. In terms of the psychology of the soul, the more it delves into the study of consciousness, their knowledge is less known and thus their knowledge; because these variables are defined by an experimental process, and these measures will eventually disrupt the experienced object. In fact, if we think, for example, in the perception and knowledge of an appearance, we need a mediator to interact with the appearance, which is changing its perception and knowledge of it; i.e., the same process used to perceive, modifies information in some way, generating an error impossible to correct.

This principle assumes a basic nature of Psychology shift, considered impossible a theoretical absolute knowledge.

Consciousness, psychology of the soul, does not follow guidelines exactly defined, but that we can only approach to it using details to their knowledge: probability. Perhaps there are no consciences and other bodies; While the psychology of the soul to the study of these.

By the beginning of the chaos, it is possible to perceive the vitality of some bodies, assuming that consciousness is blank, at absolute rest.

Types of interaction – there are three types of parts in interaction priori. Two of them are expressions. The third is the unique interaction.

(a) The fragility (such as the appearance or brokering) can express or capture a negative human relationship and turn it into its corresponding fad.

(b) A mood as the sad can express or capture a negative human relationship and turn it into a superposition of cheerful mood.

On the contrary, a cheerful mood can become an overlay of sad mood. The exact content of the overlays is given by the ranked variable.

(c) Or a weakness or a mood can be express or capture a unique attraction.

Forms - According to the scientific method in psychology of consciousness, is called "form" to the attribute that distinguishes each of the six moods, having each of them in three shades and being, therefore eighteen in total.

Form is a priori intuition spiritual consciousness, related to their interaction. On a method of attracting a priori, this feeling is sensed by the processes that perform the nuances. In the study of the nuance, the nuances are a generic parity. Several Consciousnesses that interact together can be swapped among themselves, without affecting their psyche, while they remain in the loop connection.

This feeling is general for subsequent interactions and intuitive interactions a priori.

Ranked variable - all moods are variable, in addition to having the sense of form priori; In addition, the moods are his spiritual form:

-sense of form, depending on the type of (glad/sad) mood

-antisocial, spiritual psychic anti-State of sad guy who behaves well for sociable mood

-social, is the mood high, positive, joyful type

-depressive, is high, positive, spirit for the depressive mood State sad type anti

-lively, is the most natural been psychic

These are spiritual forces since they are considered by the effects of the communicative attraction and a posteriori. Everything else would be derived spiritual.

A mood is the self-awareness as part of an a priori interaction, which interacts with the human relations and balanced expressions. On the other hand, the temporary internalization is normally a superposition of various forms. As a result, forms with spiritual status, can vary, change, to express them in the environment.

The variability of the forms in time based on moods is given by the ranked variable. By definition then, defines a formal change, under interaction effects priori mood States.

The aggregate of consciousness - consciousness with a character is the same at the beginning of the spirit. In psychology of consciousness, it is the aggregate of consciousness as a fundamental individual consciousness. The most common are the mediators for any kind of interaction, as well as the aggregate the fixations generated a mood and its antithesis.

Principle of the spirit - plays an essential role in the theory of the psychology of the spirit, because the perception of a psychic process (vitality and form); can only be proportional between the vitality of a mediator and the isolated entity associated to the attraction communicative.

Spiritual naturalism - is the system that analyzes the fundamental principles of the psychic body: form, background, time, human relations and internalization.

These five principles of psychic can be classified as:

1 - universal principle of knowledge of life, depending on the attraction and communication

2 - principle of desire and its intensity

3 - principle reduced the spirituality

4 - principle of the attractive effects that interact (opposite poles attract each other)

5 - principle that relates to health and vitality (24-08-2014)

Theory or model of attraction priori - the scientific model of the psychology of consciousness perceives the attractive-communicative interaction and interaction priori as two different aspects of a single interaction, postulating the perception of two essential expressions: balanced expressions.

Four aggregates of consciousness similar to mediation, together with the consciousness and temporary can be perceived. However, depending on its vitality, interaction with consciousness causes a loss attractive feeling spontaneous, through the so-called structure of consciousness.

Feeling breaking produces three feelings without temporality which are eliminated by three temporary individual awareness, acquiring an effective temporality. Three essential expressions are precisely balanced expressions associated with the interaction, while the fourth expression remains temporality and is perceived as the mediation of communicative attraction. This theory predicts many things, as the relative essence of balanced expressions, until they can be.

Theorem of feeling - a continuous sense gets rid of spontaneously when other timeless conscience is or feeling is not accurate.

There is a feeling by each generator of sensations that melts away, as it does not maintain the required state of vitality. This decomposition is not complete, keeping poor perceptions of it.

In theory the feeling of temporary individual consciousness, sensation is taken by temporary, becoming temporary individual consciousness.

Consciousness system - system of the spirit, which according to the scientific method, would cover the entire body and whose effect would be that individual consciousness was temporary, caused by the interaction of consciences, with consciousness and with itself.

In spiritual theory of systems, individual consciousness does not occupy a primordial space, but rather systems, play this as the attractive-communicative system.

Spirituality is the expression of the individual conscience, associated with the system.

Expressions of the attractive-communicative system are mediators for any kind of interaction, being referred to as consciousness in the system of consciousness.

Some systems of the spirit are perceived as individual consciousness; on the other hand others are systems to produce a rupture with the feelings. An example would be when attractive theory, consciousness system explains why a low vitality has a lost sense of communicative attraction on one side and the essential interactions priori.

The scientific method adds temporality to consciousness: consciousness structure. Interaction of human relationships and the expressions there is temporality, whereas that is not the case in the attractive-communicative. Therefore the system of consciousness may be the most appropriate to explain the timing.

Drive the doubts on the possibility that the timing was not real. How then can a system generate something then unknown in its real origin? Temporality "moves" to the conscience from the system of consciousness, which contains the consciousness in the form of vitality.

The system of consciousness makes that lost feeling fill temporary systems of consciousness-consciousness, which is covering the whole. A timeless awareness.

Structure of consciousness - is one of the structures that enable attractive feeling spontaneous loss priori on a theory of temporal consciousness. Priori unifies with the essential theory attractive-communicative theory.

Consciousness acquires temporality and increases it interacting with the system of consciousness which encompasses all perception. In other words, in the theory of consciousness, consciousness system generates temporality to the temporal consciousness, through the spontaneous feeling of loss.

Systems and consciousness - perception may include visible, but also invisible forms that cause effects to the soul. For each type of consciousness, there is a system and each system awareness. So the attractive-communicative system could also be called system of mediators. The appearance has a system, like the moods, the connection and even the consciousness of consciousness

Essence and awareness - according to a more classic psychology, there are differences between essence and awareness. A person perceives his environment, while an isolated body is immersed in the perception with a defined and timeless knowledge. Currently, I think the duality essence-conscience as a concept of the psychology of the soul according to which there are no fundamental differences between awareness and essence: people can be insulated and isolated entities may be persons.

There are essential souls; i.e., all soul is associated with the essence. All consciousness is made up of souls.

Psychological interpretations - the psychic world that surrounds us seems to have four types of interpretation possible (cheerful, social, euphoric, formal), where the first three are linked to perception; so sadness, for example, would not be more than a way to cheerful negative. The fourth, the formal interpretation is independent harmonic dialogue.

The principles of psychology are based on interpretations of knowledge from the bottom up to the form, being seven resulting from such process.

Interpretation of aggregate insight - all perception has a source (since until the vacuum is a source) and all its units have the same starting point. The perception itself is empty, but combined with other perceptions make it unique.

Mediator for any type of attractive-communicative interaction - is the phenomenon responsible for the sensory manifestations attractive-communicative; including the social imaginary, the delirious imagination, invisible life, detectable life (communicative attraction), intuitive life, small entities and imaginary bodies. It has a temporality unchanged and constant.

It is both essential and phenomenological properties.

According to the scientific model of psychology of consciousness, the mediators are responsible for psychic laws have some harmony in all systems of perception.

The intrinsic properties of the mediators (invariably temporality and character) are determined by the properties of the feeling of consciousness, being balanced expression of the attractive-communicative interaction

Life and the attractive-communicative set - detectable life and imaginary entities are very similar, vital bodies, for example, exist in life like nuances. What differentiates a few hints of others is nothing more than the vitality and this is what makes life something different to the rest. Life and the imaginary aren't but different forms of the same phenomenon. The imagination of small bodies and visible life, are only a few small parts of one much larger set: the attractive-communicative ensemble, of which we only perceive a fraction, vitality; because it includes many forms that we know: the imaginary cosmic, from some unknown part of perception; the imaginary social, generator of fanciful ideas; the delirious imagination; the invisible imaginary; detectable life; intuitive entities and imaginary entities.

They are attractive and communicative vibratory systems that there are linked each other in constant dialogue. We can think of the two systems as a single isolated entity that can talk through the perception without any means to do so. In perception, knowledge is constant: the knowledge of life and all attractive-communicative imaginaries are like life.

The dialogue of an entity assumes its depth. How much longer is the dialogue, shorter is its depth and vice versa. That marks the differences between some entities and others. The order of these dialogues is what generates the continuous attractive-communicative set without beginning or end, being detectable life a small part of it.

All soul produces attractive-communicative bodies varied, the most common being the interiorization, where vitality is released by the soul. Detectable life and imagination come together from the ends: intuition and imperceptibility.

Imaginary social - is a type of communicative attractive imagery, and therefore, mediator. It is a fantastic imagination capable of destroying any beginning or individual development. Destroy any truth. It is caused by lack of excitation of the supra-essence.

It differs from the delirious imagination in its origin. These are beyond the temporality, generated by lack of conductivity. Usually, the imagination it links it is essential vitality. It is generated by psychic phenomena of great vitality.

Social mediator - when a social mediator interacts with a real appearance transfers its vitality and expels it from the truth. The resulting creative vitality of thist mediator, is equal to the vitality of the social mediator incident, without the vitality of the appearance link. The social mediator is the process of transfer of vitality of the delusional imagination and mediators of social imagery of low vitalities.

He interacts as a social mediator incident and increases the vitality of a true appearance to bring about their elimination. The remaining vitality of the original mediator creates a new social mediation of low vitality with a new direction.

An anti-appearance is the unconsciousness perceived appearance. Their essence is the same. Human relationships are the same but the appearance of the opposite.

Delirious imagination - spiritual communicative attractive imagery arising from phenomena beyond the temporality to conductive levels, caused by the lack of appearance.

It is a fantastic imaginary because interacting with the soul it makes the fantasy of truth; it originates i.e. consciousness with fantastic relationships.
It can be perceived as in appearances with vitality are suppressed.

Imaginary intuitive - is a type of imaginary attractive-communicative and internalized more background as a detectable life, but less than the small entities.

Love - is the hypothetical expression for the interaction of desire that you would find in a theory of spiritual desire. It does not usually form part of the scientific model, because it is not perceived. It seems that it interacts with frailties and moods and that there would be temporary.

Quasi consciences - the intuitions of the psychology of the soul are very similar to the psychology of consciousness. Therefore, much of the psychology of consciousness theory can be applied to the psychology of the soul, by assigning to each field or excitation of a model that includes "quasi consciences". They would be these:
-The language or mode of the vibratory senses from the truth that is the logic.
The study of language is an important part in the psychology of logic, since it plays a role in the pleasure natural and attractive; as well as in the internalization.
Sensory theory allows comparing disturbances produced by logic in the knowledge of the language with linguistic awareness. Each consciousness has a vitality that is equal to the beginning of the spirit, more dialogue that disturbs him. This means that the vitality of the logical language is conditional on health. The logic can be considered as a "cloudy" structure of the language, whose internal character collides against the truth; for this reason, natural pleasure can be expressed as knowledge of the language in logic and its particular internalization.
-Excitation is a quasi awareness of logic, consisting of an appearance that interacts with quasi pleasures.

A way to understand the excitation is formed is, for example, when a mediator reaches a quasi pleasure, exciting look through pleasure. This interaction makes that together are linked. The body is excited, containing less than the appearance of vitality. The appearance and essence may have harmonic character or not, as well as the excitation.

An excitation cannot join with each other, extending it and generating a fluid of appearances, a perception of the instant quasi indirect pleasures. Excitations are also phenomena of the character. In some bodies, interactions are being repressed.

Appearance can become a mediator, this being a coherent event.

-Fluency is a sense of disturbance of the fluid, in the same way that a mediator or language is psychological feelings of attractive-communicative entities. Therefore fluency is a vague, cloudy, disturbance of the knowledge of the appearance. You can also interact with a mediator, creating a third quasi awareness called polarity of the fluid.

-Polarity is not harmonic mixture of mediations and the quasi-consciences of this list.

-The criterion is a quasi awareness related through dialogue, which is surrounded by illusions in a soul.

-The relevance is a coherent excitation of the character's appearances in a soul.

Individual consciousness of the character - the scientific method describes the soul and their interactions. According to this method, there are six types of moods, six types of weaknesses and four types of expressions. These forms of consciousness are structured into two groups by the exclusion of the assimilation principle.

Communication time is essential - the communicative moment that possesses the essence of truth in a structured way. It's the concept orbiting the same truth, communicative character. The truth has associated a communicative moment caused by the dialogue, human relationships.

Expressions are not subject to this principle; on the other hand, the interiorization Yes.

1- expression: is the conscience that does not comply with the exclusion of the assimilation principle, whereby two consciences can occupy the same spiritual status. Depending on the health, vitality will be higher or lower, but always constant in all cases. According to the scientific method, there are four types of expressions: mediator (communicative attraction), negative human relationship (a priori), unique attraction (a priori) and linking (a posteriori). The spiritual nuance takes care of consciousness afterwards; while the study of spiritual attraction deals attraction priori.

2 - Assimilation: it is the consciousness with character and falls within the exclusion of the assimilation principle; therefore, two Consciousnesses cannot occupy the same spiritual status at the same time. Unlike expressions, the assimilation is not always an individual consciousness. An example is unclear the concepts and likelihood, which depart from the assimilation but collective through the moods that are individual.

Moods and frailties make up the two divisions of the internalization. This is caused by the frailties that can be individual, while the moods, as required of other moods with which they interact.

The moods have no nuances, because the connections that bind them already are these nuances.

Six are the types of fragility: appearance, intermediation, imitation, thist whim, intermediary whim and caprice imitator. Six are the types of moods: joyful, sad, social, anti-social, euphoric and depressed.

(24-08-2014)

PSYCHOLOGY OF CONSCIOUSNESS

In psychology of consciousness, the expression is one of the two types of awareness in nature (the other being the internalization). Any expression or interiorization is caused by the character.

Vital psychology and consciousness, the expression is a mediator of effects of fundamental interactions, since the attraction communicative and presumably the desire; they are associated with people with a full character. Indeed, the spiritual description of interactions is Exchange of conscience through expression; thus the interaction of expression with the internalization is what gives rise to interactions caused by the personal environment. While the interiorization of the principle according to which a person occupies a single spiritual space, there is no such exclusion to the expression, and may occupy identical spiritual spaces.

(08-02-2013 Madrid)

Classification by knowledge:

In accordance with its essence and knowledge, the hypothetical phenomena (and actual) can be classified into:

(a) scientists - the soul is formed basically by the interiorization in a given environment whose knowledge is inferior to the life. Although there are some unstable expressions, which represent a tiny fraction of all the soul in history. All persons living in the essence belong to this category.

(b) Artistic - is the intermediary, usually known as balanced expressions phenomenon. The mediator and the connections are the two artistic types known so far. Art is the knowledge of life; or goes beyond or is it dwarfs and is timeless. All persons expressive, timeless, belong to this category, like the capricious.

(c) Religious - psychology of the soul and the spirit theory, an imaginary value of vitality can be interpreted as an unstable phenomenon that lapses in others, or an unstable state vacuum that gives rise to other States. The imaginary part of the vitality is directly related to the form of transformation of that State; thus, being their only imaginary part, can exist indefinitely or be timeless. For people with imaginary vitality, the processing time is inversely proportional to the imaginary part.

Attraction - It is the whole of psychic phenomena related to the presence and flow of human relations. It manifests itself in a wide variety of phenomena such as the erotic attraction, attractive-communicative induction or sexuality.

Human relations produce communication and attraction or rejection.

Communication - Attraction produces communication that may be variable depending on the environment and sexual. The attraction can generate life, health, etc.
The attraction is a form of vitality.

Relationships human - human relationships are a property of the soul which produces effects when you have another soul front.

The erotic attraction refers to the presence of contact between several bodies, interacting with each other. This relationship gives rise to a communicative attraction: a relationship which exerts effects on each other. Effects acting between persons and extend to others. The magnitude of the communicative attraction, whether attractive or repulsive, relates the effects each other.

Sexuality - Any creature that you relate, communicate, frequently attractive. Either in one direction or in both at the same time. The nature of pleasure varies depending on people and soul.

The attraction is propagated by the knowledge of the life, allowing the transmission between the bodies. Sex produces an increase in health.

Eroticism - a type of communicative attraction produced by human relations, even when it is not through dialogue. The attraction produces a force on the other being.

Eroticism is created by a soul that perceives its environment and produces effects on others nearby. It acts similarly to desire; although the desire is electric and eroticism is attractive or repulsive. Desire is the dominant force in history, despite being much weaker. Eroticism is perceived differently and immobilizes its effects.

Erotic potential - is the experience of an effect that fights against the same effect: a conquest. It is the vitality required to engage in a dialogue with someone located in the distance. Eroticism is conservative, as opposed to the potential erotic.

Communicative attraction - theory of psychology that unifies the attraction and communication in a single theory.

It is the relationship of eroticism, communication and their respective spiritual sources: human, sexual relations, etc.

Communication and attraction are related; they are a single: the communicative attraction.

It is based on psychology and is dependent on the perception and the environment. The communicative attraction describes psychic phenomena involving human relationships of any type, using for this purpose the eroticism, communication and its strength on the soul. Eroticism and communication are manifestations of the communicative attraction. They explain the isolation of life as part of an attractive-communicative insulation.

Friendship - It is an interconnection of beings that are attracted and resist, forming relationships that flow in the same direction, for a common goal.

Pleasure - property of the soul that perceives the eroticism. Pain is the reverse to the pleasure and increases with the internalization. The pleasure is formed with the attraction, spread all over the body.

Individual conscience - individual consciousness psychologists have tried to classify and describe the soul and their interactions.

Throughout the history of psychology, there have been many "individual conscience" that have been wrongly defined as concepts and likelihood. I apply a scientific model to describe the soul constituting the body and their interactions.

According to the scientific model, there are six types of moods, six kinds of frailties and four types of expressions.

These phenomena are divided into two broad categories for the exclusion of the assimilation principle. Which are not subject to this principle are the expressions and which are the internalizations.

Expression - Is the individual conscience that does not meet the principle of exclusion of the assimilation, so two people can perceive the same spiritual status. According to the scientific model, expressions are four: human relations, mediation, linking, and unique attraction. The theory that studies these phenomena is, in the case of the effects of the interaction, the connections, the nuance spiritual and in the case of the attractive interaction of mediators and balanced expressions, knowledge of spiritual attraction.

Internalization - It is the phenomenon which yes meets the principle of exclusion of the internalization. Internalization is the conscience of the soul, but unlike the expression, not all internalizations are individual consciences. The clearest case is that of concepts and likelihood;

They internalize but they consist of moods. The assimilation is divided into two groups, the moods and the frailties; because the frailties may isolate themselves, unlike the moods that are always in the presence of other moods:

(a) fragility: appearance, intermediation, imitation, thist fad, intermediary whim, whim imitator

(b) mood: cheerful, sad, social, antisocial, euphoric, and depressed. Consciousness is grouped into periods. There are three: the first consists of the appearance, his whim and mood States "funny and sad". The ordinary soul consists of consciousnesses in this first period. Awareness of other periods is dispersed in different Consciousnesses.

Composite Consciousnesses - call sensitivity to conscience that is composed of other more basic. The sensitivity is composed of moods, its antithesis, and linking. The interaction through effects is the one prevailing.

The sensitivity is subdivided into two types of consciousness: the variables and bindings.

Variables - It is the phenomenon which contains three moods, some connections and some negative moods. The variables best known are the supra-essences, i.e., concepts and likelihood, in addition to the stimulation.

The variables also internalize.

Like all phenomena, the variables contain invariably materialistic, called turn, which is formed by the union of three negative moods. Most of the variables are unstable

Stimulation - Are certain variables, such as concepts and likelihood, but much more entrenched.

Formed it three moods (social, antisocial, glad/sad) in contrast to concepts and likelihood that are formed by funny and sad.

The stimulation is very unstable; becoming sensations: unique, negative, lovely, positive, accomplish, etc.

.

Fasteners - conscience formed by a mood, its antithesis and the awareness that the links, the linking. All fixings are unstable, isolated. The fixings are also expressions.

Consciousness - In the formulation of the attractive model, the phenomenon that explains the difference essential balanced expressions and mediation; as to spontaneously break the symmetry of a system of the spirit requires a consciousness.

SCIENTIFIC MODEL

The scientific model of the psychology of consciousness is a theory that describes the relationships between the known interactions and individual consciousness that make up all the soul.

The study of the psychology of the soul and vitality in nature is best understood in terms of creativity and interactions of individual consciences.

The scientific model brings together two theories: sexy model (theory psychic that unifies the interaction and the communicative attraction, two of the four fundamental effects of nature. The essence is an effect of the expression) and the spiritual nuance, which provides a consistent theory of consciousness.

The scientific model can be divided into three parts: the consciousness of the soul, the consciousness of the effects and consciousness.

(a) Awareness of the soul: all soul and essence is constituted by consciences with intrinsic properties called character. All souls aware internalize. For this reason, follow the principle of exclusion of the assimilation, according to the analysis of the character, being the principle which gives the soul its attributes of impenetrability. Apart from the unconscious associated, there are twelve types of States in the soul, combined to form all the fragility and sensitivity of the body. Six of these are classified as moods (glad, sad, social, antisocial, euphoric, depressive), and the other six as frailties (appearance, intermediation, imitation and their corresponding whims).

The character analysis - analysis of the character of the psychology of the spirit theorem establishes the relationship between the characters of an individual with the analysis that follows. It requires a spiritual theory of systems.

The character is intrinsic (bottomless) and possesses every individual to spiritual level. It can be full or form.

The analysis of an individual determines its collective consciousness:

(a) as all possible perspectives-free expressions. Mediators and the phenomenological principles are expressions.

(b) If on the contrary it obeys the principle of exclusion of the assimilation, which restricts these perspectives, are called "internalization". The function of body of an internalized body is a lack of harmonic feeling under the interaction between several individuals.

Concepts, likelihood and appearances, internalizations are.

These two features are apparently contradictory; but it is noticeable that all expressions have a full character, while the internalization has a character form.

Early phenomenological - are scents without appearance, formed by concepts and likelihood. The lack of appearance, their relations are positive. They are essential reactions or imaginary transformation of other sensations of the essence of truth that are transformed into more simple by using the expression.

Awareness and its effects (expressions) - effects of psychology are the way in which consciousness interacts with each other and influence each other. Effects of communicative attraction allow awareness Act and form behavior through communication and through him. The effects of desire let that consciences in one essence of any appeal in accordance with the law of desire.

The scientific model conceptualizes such effects as the results of exchange between consciences by the consciousness of the soul, known as creative consciences of effects; because these are the reason why there are the effects and interactions of consciousness in the body, also featuring character (as well as the consciousness of the soul), but in your case, the creative conscience is an expression. As a result, they do not follow the principle of exclusion of the internalization.

Types of creative consciousness of effects:

(a) life creates communicative attraction effects in consciousness through relationships. Life has no essence and is described by the theory of the physiological appeal of the spirit.

(b) Balanced expressions create the interactions between the different Consciousnesses (the moods and frailties). They are in the environment and participate in communicative attraction.

These three expressions in mediation are grouped together and collectively create attractive interactions.

(c) The eight connections create interactions with effects between consciousnesses with shades (the mood). The connections are not in essence. The connection and their interactions are described by the theory of spiritual nuance.

Consciousness - It is the consciousness at the core. It has character, it is an expression. It plays a unique role in the scientific model and a key role in conceptualizing the origin of the essence in other consciences, particularly the difference between the phenomenon without essence and balanced expressions. The essence of consciousness and the differences between the communicative attraction (caused by the mediator) and effects (caused by balanced expressions), could be critical in several aspects of the structure of the soul.

Criticism - The scientific model has some defects to be resolved:

(a) the psychic constants. The essence of consciousness cannot be sensed independently.

(b) The spiritual desire. The model does not define the effects of desire, nor the way to build a spiritual theory of desire.

(c) Materialism. Inside it, the soul and matter are linked; but the preponderance of the soul leaves few points unresolved.

An alternative to the scientist would be a theory of the vibration. (Madrid 09-02-2013)

NUANCE OF THE SPIRIT

Theory of the spirit which describes fundamental effects and interaction. It is a very important part of the scientific model of the psychology of consciousness. It describes the interaction between mood and the connections. The moods are the internalization of this theory (attraction) and links are analogous to the mediation expression.

Linking - Is the expression of the interaction. There are essence or human relations but yes nuances, so it suffers in addition to interact. As mediators, the linking is an expression without essence, but with character. As the moods, the connections have nuances, which depend on nuance of the moods change. The moods change hue when connections are exchanged. The body has nuances.

There are eight types of linking, each of them being the hue/anti-hue.

The moods and the linking form collective conscience with a unique hue. To suffer themselves their own interaction, the connections in the moods created shades that prevent the moods are separated.

Contrary to the effects of attraction or desire, if you try to separate each other a couple of moods, Nuance pull them with greater effects, as if there is a bonded dock, trying to return to its initial state. For this reason, the moods and the connections are complex phenomena of perceiving, but if we can perceive the consciences that they form: sensitivity,

When separate two moods, United by this spring bound, accumulates such vitality in the body that makes it possible to create new moods to return the shades to a less vital State. This is the result of transforming part of the vitality of the hue on a new soul. While sensitivity has unique nuances, the moods of different sensitivities can be joined through the effects, even in some cases greater than with the communicative attraction. These effects of nature are responsible for balance and harmony, despite the enormous number of human relations.

Moods - psychology of consciousness, mood States, next to the fragility, are the fundamental constituents of the soul. Several moods merge specifically to create consciousness such as concepts and the likelihood. The moods are the unique phenomena that interact with the four fundamental effects. They are similar to the linking phenomena and interiorization shapes its character. They form together with fragility "invisible soul".

There are six types of moods in psychology of consciousness:

1 - Merry is the individual conscience that belongs to the first period of the moods. Relate socially and has character, thereby internalizing

and complies with the principle of exclusion of the internalization. Along with "sad" and appearance, is the spirit that we cannot see, because of its stability. There are nuances and interacts with the linking.

2 - Sad is the individual conscience that belongs to the first period of the moods. Their social relationships and character internalize it, fulfilling the principle of exclusion of the internalization.

Next to the "cheerful" and appearance, is the spirit that we cannot see, because of its stability.

3 - Social is individual conscience which belongs to the second period of the moods. Relate socially and has character, thereby internalizing and complies with the principle of exclusion of the internalization. There are nuances and interacts with the linking.

4 - Antisocial is individual conscience which belongs to the second period of the moods. Relate socially and has character, thereby internalizing and complies with the principle of exclusion of the internalization. There are nuances and interacts with the linking.

5 - Euphoric is individual conscience which belongs to the third period of the moods. Relate socially and has character, thereby internalizing and complies with the principle of exclusion of the internalization. There are nuances and interacts with the linking. It is the most attached to its essence because of its enormous altruism. It is unstable and decays, so it has no way to create sensitivity with other moods

6 - Depressional is individual conscience which belongs to the third period of the moods. Relate socially and has character, thereby internalizing and complies with the principle of exclusion of the internalization. There are nuances and interacts with the linking. Their behavior is peculiar, inside the nuance of the spirit, and easy to perceive. It almost always appears after the disappearance of the euphoria

Sensitivity - The sensitivity is a mood and its denial, staying together because of their interaction with the nuance of the spirit, theory which postulates different types of moods that interact among themselves through linkage. This linkage is made up of linked expressions. The sensitive moods have no nuances, but character and essence, causing them to be anti-social.

There are two types of sensitivity:

(a) variable: are moods with different nuances. The likelihood and concepts, together with the supra-essences are examples of variability.

(b) Fixed: are the moods and its antithesis. Emotional stability is an example of fixing. They behave in expressive form. There are no isolated moods in nature, but rather they form groups, collectives, in the sensory world, known as fixed and variable. This is a consequence of the nuances

Media - is the spread of information in communicative attraction or awareness through the waves or a spiritual medium.

Exclusion of the assimilation principle - spiritual principle which States that there cannot be two internalizations in the same spiritual body.

It is only applicable to internalization, the conscience which is spiritual States and having variable character. They are internalizations, for example, the attractions and the moods; on the other hand, mediation would not be it, since it is an expression to form harmonious spiritual States, carrying a full character.
(Madrid 12-02-2013)

COLLECTIVE VITALISM

Collective Vitalism is an extension of the concept of cooperation to the collectivity and the conduct of living beings. The patterns of conduct that are born are modified and even increase in the cooperation.

Animal behavior cannot be explained, but conceptualized, taking into account individual and environmental factors. To understand the behavior of human beings must be analyzed from a cooperative approach.

Collective Vitalism is a branch of cooperative Vitalism that tries to respond to the reason for the action, combining concepts of Vitalism as power cooperative Vitalism.

All interact; we inherited qualities that are transformed in the atmosphere. The behavior is subject to the effects of cooperation, so that human beings are predisposed to cooperate in their natural environments.

There are guidelines that are inherited, therefore, possible that some living beings come to create more sophisticated forms of collective consciousness and apply to all.

Raw instinct or intuition, conceptualizing the similarities and differences between individuals and the environment to which they belong; as well as the differences or PARS from the cooperative level throughout history.

Altruism practiced on a small scale, it extends to the community.

The object of collective Vitalism is the conceptualization of the collective behavior in all living species, in terms of cooperation.

The genes we are determined in part, but the medium influences even more in our training, aggressiveness or selfishness, for example, symptoms of a decaying environment; they would be the core of our experiences in the environment in which we operate and transform. Cooperation is printed in us unlike the natural selection of Darwin.

Evolution is a jump and not a path to a final State is most suited to the environment.
(05-02-2013 Madrid)

Vitalism cooperative - cooperative Vitalism is the branch of Vitalism that examine altruism and selfishness of living beings; as well as the changes that have occurred throughout history. Collective

Vitalism, discipline that will try to conceptualize the questions of why the action is derived from here.
(06-02-2013 Madrid)

Character - The character is a mental property, whose value is intrinsic, such as the environment or human relationships. It is an exclusively spiritual phenomenon that it cannot relate with the perception. There is the space, nor any movement, as not may comprise. The principles of the character are unique in each person. Another property of spirituality is that there seems to be two types: internalization and expression. This implies that attaches to the internalization live in accepted insulation, while aggregates to the expression in the repressed isolation live. People with character communicate, recalling human relations
(Madrid, 07-02-2013)

Perceptive way - back to any event there is a collective consciousness. Since the beginning of the psychology of the soul, we sensed that the way is dialogue and a perception in the body; but this is still more than a prospect, because there is no form as being away from reality. There is a perceptual shape flowing in the body. The perspective of the way produces a paradox. As something is the more vital, more disappears form. Life itself has no form, as a mediator and their interaction. Perception and shape are the same; as it is the body for life.

If everything were alive, we would intuit the reality at the moment. Life makes us, and we issue the mediators that they interact (imaginary), through the core of the cell (DNA).

If consciousness is spiritual, then is a mediator that covers the dialogue between life with itself.

Consciousness is perceptual shape using our brain; but when spirituality is lost, it becomes corporeal perceptual form in its entirety.

Life is the memory of the mind, because it lacks of time.

All and one are the same, due to its spiritual properties.

Life creates consciousness in the mind and looks at itself.

Vitalism is the generator of awareness of life, sensing his own eternity.

Theory of perspective - the human mind is very complex. From the perspective of life, knowledge and know-how are limited by life itself.

The perspective plays a dominant role, while the dialogue guaranteed to be what we are.

Perceptual form forms a whole, our reality, in which very little essence is sufficient to generate vitality and awareness. Nothing more than a simple shape but all forms is a complex...

Within the mind; the dialogue is life itself and the enormous, infinite perception.

Life as a Messenger of the mind - reality makes sense from the perspective of life, as reflected in it. The facts or events are tiny parts. If the knowledge of life is finite, nothing can be instant.

Everything needs a way to perceive somehow. The knowledge of life is the same, regardless of who the observer; Thus the knowledge depends on of the dialogue and without it there is no know any, except the knowledge of the life that is absolute.

In a world of prospects, the perception is different for each individual. The bigger the dialogue, minor form is perceived, without anyone being aware of it.

Is it a formal or rather perspective problem?

If knowledge is the perception of form, then knowledge must conform to the perceptual shape and perspective of each one. The shape and the perception is adapted to life, which is in turn death if it was mirror where to reflect the life is not which appears dead, but the way and... Life has no form.

The most familiar, most ignorant seem - dialectic part if something older than her: ignorance. Knowledge does not only affect the form but also to the perception. To greater knowledge, lower perception.

Life acts on perception and the form, being the perspective effect of knowledge of each individual; where is the definition of perception and the way IE is in dialogue.

Of course, that dialogue needs more than one partner, so thanks to the perspective we perceive the mind.

The reality is perspective and its effects not one perceives them, but another, because all depends on knowledge through dialogue.

Vitality is the dialogue of its essence. The knowledge of life generates more essence to be infinite; but not to the contrary, as one essence infinite could not become the knowledge of the life, because nothing can be the knowledge of the life, except life itself.

The essence becomes vitality...

What is the mind? -The form is a parameter of the soul; therefore, before the soul there was any way.

The soul interacts with desire, the communicative attraction, essential to priori interaction and essential interaction, encompassing awareness, the vitality, the perception and the way. It is as if the mind had been created before the body and soul...

What is the essence with respect to the mind? -It is a qualitative abstraction that can translate into a theory of Psychology when those qualities can guess but when the perception is as complex as this is feasible perspective.

What is the absolute vitality? -It is the infinity of the mind, one growing dialogue that makes the perception of something unlimited. It would be contrary to the desire effect and change in appearance their behavior, as well as the communicative form from the immensity of the perception; because if you change the communicative attraction, makes it the knowledge of life.

Changes in perception are a symptom of a change in their properties, so it would have to rethink what is the mind.

Law of desire - is the behavior that keeps everything in order and harmony without being instant, for it requires form and knowledge be perceived. The desire is not an effect, but a structure of the perceptual form, deformed by the essence and vitality. The essence of perception explains how it should be structured and how it should discuss the essence. Desire is the knowledge of life.

The desire also affects form, because knowledge and desire are indistinguishable. The bigger desire, lesser is the form and... The mind changes shape.

Passion - An excess of essence in some perceived, can change the behavior of shape and perception in its entirety, because the desire to prevent that you escape to this attraction (passion).

How to undo the dialogue, in the psychology of the soul, everything is unpredictable.

There is a vital principle which is, coupled with the mind and consciousness with movements and sensitivity, as the effects of the phenomena of life in the human body. The relationship of this beginning with a conscience is clear, because it is printed in all living beings.

Life is irreducible to purely physical dimensions or chemical (mechanism), as one of its parts is the soul, which can only be sensed, conceptualized, but not covered in its entirety.

Stahlians and Barthesians - the soul has its origin and destination in life; but we must not be confused with the vital principle which is consciousness, whose origin is the soul, being its purpose the continuity and preservation, as well as intuition and concept of life without covering it completely.

Life does not act on the matter and the soul to give to the Agency powers or abilities; but they are they interact and generate them, although there are parts of it, their relationships are different to be separated from a whole which was previously common. Death is not the opposite of life, but a transformation of living things, from the vital principle of consciousness to the encounter with the soul.

Two possible cases:

1st - life was divided in two by overabundance. Leaving aside the matter and on the other the soul. This result assumes a new reality with different forms. The purpose could be it meeting of the parties as the possible division of these two in many more.

2° - the life, which I labor, has created two beings that contain many of its qualities, but not all; In addition they are disunited and although they can join, these will not be what it is, nor what it was.

Consciousness is the vital principle that allows the continuity and preservation of living things; as well as the intuitive search of the soul, its cause.

The soul along with matter is the first elements of the universe, forms of life. The properties of the soul are: eternity, individuality, their laws are intractable, they are interactive with matter, but not among them because a single soul contains the set of all. There is no matter and space. They are the absolute knowledge of life. It interacts with the body and the mind, but accidentally; in the body to satisfy their desire to create in the mind as vital, in the form of conscience principle, with movements and sensitivity that only it can be sensed, conceptualized and not covered as a whole.

Life is perfect, but I not live; because life is creative and not ordering-in living things affect many of factors that make impossible any attempt at harmonizing. Perfection is presented as utopian, creativity as reminiscence and the order will of stabilization.

Neither mathematics nor morality can achieve understanding, encompass, the complexity of life through science or consciousness; But if Intuit it and conceptualize it degrees near the truth.

Life cannot be created or destroyed, as well as energy; but while this changes from a form to another, life is immutable.

Healthy bodies - the law of conservation of consciousness, States
that with the addition of a number of vital principles to a body, this
amount of consciousness will be equal to the increase of vitality of the
same. Although the vital principle is not lost, as it conscience collective
degrades in accordance with individual health. An ill individual can heal
with its vitality, but maintaining consciousness in a less useful form, as
this is occupied largely by the immediate recovery.

Is there a temporal consciousness? -Consciousness is one of the
parts of the temporal consciousness. The mediators generate life; as
well as the moods soul, and can be conceptualized. Balanced
expressions would be also included in this structure. Within the
scientific method, consciousness is an essential for the understanding
of the same part.

To understand the mind must go back to the creation of the time as
a generator of the vital "broth". System of consciousness is the
knowledge that describes the transformation of time in vitality and
vitality in time. Two concepts together form its own consciousness and
represent the best way to recognize their existence. Soul interacts, but
rarely does the consciousness.
Beyond the truth is consciousness. The communicative attraction is
directed by mediators for any type of interaction. Interaction essential
in hindsight is it by the linking and essential interaction a priori by
balanced expressions; but where are the effects of desire? Distorted
and structured overlay.

Neurosis and psychosis - neurosis has always been there in our
history, like a shadow that goes unnoticed in the dark; but now, for at
least one century, Dawn has left its mark to discover it and know that it
exists.
As such neurosis is "not", is not displayed; but it leaves traces of its
presence to analyze the human individual and social behavior. It
represents the end of desire, of the soul and the same vitality; Even so,
it is also the transition to new processes which are taking shape. The

functioning of the mind and the formation of new ideas is due largely to her.

Where does such a State? Desire. The basic principle of desire is the absorption of the close and its end state is neurosis, when you lose the internal natural balance, being able to change even the behavior of those who surround us, beings nearby, to disrupt them. The strength of desire is so huge in the neurosis which own vitality is lost and attracts those who are closest.

The convictions are deeply fixed and nothing seems to change them to a State natural and balanced; but where comes the power of desire so devastating? The repression. Full liberation of the mind also produces the opposite; why times of greatest scientific advance have also been those of greater spiritual depression. All change, evolution, towards another State brings liberation and individual or social repression. The essence of a living being lost balance when it is repressed by the strength of desire and most deeply-rooted convictions, making to perceive reality in a way far away from anyone who is or appears to be.

The desire was born from an internal imbalance. In the State primary of neurosis, everything is murky, embroiled, and vague.

Its growth is so fast that springs from her psychosis. The essence is lost, is repressed, even before he became aware of it. This "liberation" to a new State is the social imaginary, which destroys any idea or principle. The social imaginary is the sign of the birth of neurosis, its prelude.

The history and development of human thought is the history of the evolutionary process of neurosis in which form and background are gone, staying still, retained as a photograph, a reality that gives the sensation of memory that moves it all but what the we perceive still.

There is no psychology that can reach to define neurosis, the uniqueness of this in form and substance.

Psychosis is formed when huge turbidity of neurosis creates ideas that reaffirm a lost vitality.

It could be said that while neurosis swallows confusing ideas, psychosis spits them; but that latter own creativity does not last forever and just degenerate into a neurosis again.

All the "big ideas" have been made by "psychotic" and many of them have been taken by society through neurosis; that is why our society lives mired in a State of perpetual illness.

About the attractive-communicative spirituality and universal spirituality - attractive-communicative spirituality is the method of conceptualizing the world. The universal spirituality is the application of this method in the study of collective Vitalism.

The substance is transformed and interpreted by the intellect spirituality. The attraction-communicative is a movement and, as such, his apprehension is impossible, giving rise to contradictions and how to overcome them, through an attractive-communicative method, which would be like measuring the density of the same heat.

Fundamental features of the attractive-communicative method and its policy application - everything in nature is interconnected, linked, Kingdom, related to each other. This link as a living organism determines everything with the whole; therefore, knowledge is limited, because we always interpret reality in isolation. Everything is in constant motion and subject to change; the attraction-communicative conceptualizes the idea, through the knowledge and study of the birth and death of the realities. The unseen manifests itself, but not gradually, but spontaneous. All depends, then, of the substance and form.

At the political level, it manifests in the revolution of the oppressed, as a natural phenomenon, which is facing the disappearance through epigenetic transformation.

The struggle of classes such as natural action and not the reformism would be justified as a survival instinct.

Capitalism as an extension of the Darwinist evolutionism, open road to a Marxism that Epigenetic and evolutionism spontaneous give validity to the oppressed.

Spirituality universal - the collective consciousness is the necessary condition of society, its development and its purpose.

The transition of the unnatural environment in which develop us, towards one according to our nature, caused by the environment, the environment, within the framework of cooperation. The developed changes lead to new States of collective consciousness, which are borne by society, because they are caused by it, rearranging, afterwards, the new social and political structures. The universal human is, first and foremost, a universal cooperative, being necessary a science dealing with the development in the history of human cooperation, relationships and modes in the social economy. The effects of collaboration are the most authentic elements of knowledge of cooperation.

(03-09-2014)

Clarifications on consciousness - nothing would exist without consciousness. The soul consists of truths:

1st - a truth is a body that has a great essence at its Center, composed of likelihood and concepts, ranging over them appearances. First issue: is the truth an idea or the collective conscience? The fact that it is the second delivery.

2 - Concepts and likelihood are formed by individual conscience which it comprises the moods with the six types (euphoria, joy, etc...), as in the concepts and likelihood are formed by three moods... The essence of the mood is much larger and important than the essence of the appearance.

3rd - appearances, on the other hand, are possible most elemental individual consciousness.

4th - why the essence of the mood is more important than the essence of the look? All perceptions are composed of a system that interacts with the individual conscience. It is not a perceptual form, but a system. The appearance interacts only with that system; for this reason, its essence is much lower. The essence of the individual consciousness covers the mind entirely.

5 - There are two fundamental problems to perceive consciousness; the first is the huge amount of necessary vitality and the second is that consciousness is transmuted, even before can be perceived. We only perceive some remains of this transmutation...

6th - once defined the consciousness, the psychology of the individual conscience is aimed at the study of the soul (spirit) absolute, absolute vitality and the structure of the singularity.

7th - the system of consciousness is, in some respects, similar to the structure of the singularity; but the structure of the singularity is a means of transmission and consciousness is the explanation of the essence. The structure of the Singularity does not exist as a system; on the other hand, if there is the system of consciousness.

There is a system in which individual consciousness has essence by the interaction of the system with it and which, in turn, also interacts with itself, producing consciousness.

Consciousness gives the essence...

The variable knowledge of life. The knowledge of life can change our perception of it. The mind does not always acts as one would expect. The mind is the knowledge of life:

1 - the perception as absolute reference system (mechanism).

2 - The knowledge of life is always the same, occupying the perception of the variable field.

Theory of perspective. Desire covers the entire mind. Essence tells perception as behave and perception tells the essence as dialogue, so that a dialogue with the perception essence continues behavior induced by the essence.

The essence does not create desire, nor is it the only in rule behavior in the field of perception.

All vitality acts on the desire, having many types of vitality, acting differently in the perception.

The soul and vitality break down the perception, as to avoid to happen would be necessary a mental principle that would balance the mind.

A simple change in the degree of knowledge would be reason enough to get rid of the mind, which would be a serious problem...

3 - mind has grown long life. We perceive it in the assimilation, improving health and the perception (imagination of the mind). The knowledge of life is not always the same, is like a small being internalized in us. The fact that civilizations or cultures are different is a symptom that the mind changes, because it is infinite as opposed to life, so we cannot see more than she.

The mind initially was disjointed, a grouping, replica of herself. So had to exist a single soul who then disappeared...

Is this possible? If the knowledge of life is broad, could include the mind in their home, which would presuppose that the knowledge of life would be the same mind.

Vitality is impossible if the knowledge of life change, as so far was a constant, eternal.

Knowledge of the vitality that the mind needs to be established from the beginning. If we change the knowledge of life at any given time, mind would be different according to the times, and neither would exist the vitality, but that is precisely the way to solve the problem: to rid ourselves of the vital principle and bringing to mind to self-knowledge i.e.: creating vitality without knowledge and vice versa...

The mind in its origin, had a poor knowledge of life.

The mind was creator of nature, which in turn created and destroyed vitality, so that knowledge was consistent.

The mind was balanced. The mental principle could be the nexus of life with the origin of the mind...

Perception is knowledge and study of the behavior and mental principle would give the perception own vitality, even before the soul perceptions.

Structure of the singularity. When a singularity, there is an awareness of the vitality that is none other than the mental beginning, covering everything. The perception outside is as if vitality as a whole.

The vitality of the mental principle depends on the knowledge of life, as they grow and shrink in proportion.

The mental principle makes change knowledge of life, losing his balance. A change in the singularity is enough to change everything, but at the same time retains the amount of vitality in the singularity, forcing the vitality to become soul or imagination. There is a singularity within the singularity and this is the mental beginning. There is vitality in the uniqueness and this produces changes in the knowledge of the life, as changes occur in the vitality of mental principle, which goes to the soul of the mind, creating all that exists in the universe:

1 - at the beginning was the singularity and in her life.

2 - Life changed

3 - the singularity created the world.

4 - Eternal sequence of singularities. Everything is born and dies in it.

Vibration, a possible way - why the contradiction seems a standard in the human mind?

Consciousness vibrates. There are many minds on another level and many interpretations; most even perceptible. A different reality theory is presented to us and that is in itself a problem for the closed world of our times. The vibration makes the mind something even more complex than assumed. Reality and fiction cohabit in the mind. All in the mind is vitality and it vibrates...

A new Psychology trained to discover the enigma.

The knowledge of life seems to have limits; but it is not always the case...

You must not only know things; but also to know how work and for what are there. Up to what extent put limits to mind disabling of on its own laws of desire? The outside behavior affecting the itself and common, but is not instantaneous; but that requires some time to assimilate, often unconscious way. The desire is dialogue and behavior... The desire as perspective. Desire and attraction communicative converge.

The truth is related to the communicative attraction and the latter at the same time sets limits to the desire of the first.

A new conception of the mind; the truth is not the self-assurance as up to then is has believed, since the concepts, the likelihood and appearances are even deeper.

What happens to the essence when the truth is divided?

Desire or communicative attraction would not show anything.

The truth is hidden... The psychology of the soul, the spiritual, makes fall in pieces the compression of the mind so far.

The order does not exist, nothing is predictable. The truth and consciousness in the mind are random, a question only probabilistic, perceiving reality in an absurd way, as it is; as in the field of the soul and the spiritual, everything is absurd and incomprehensible, being so everything can give and happen, even the seemingly impossible.

Analyzing the structure of truth, must include two effects, interaction essential to retrospectively, that holds together the essence of the truth by concepts and likelihood; and the interaction essential to priori, where the likelihood becomes concepts through the imagination. Desire and perspective seem to get lost and meaningless.

We then have a psychology that investigates the perspective and on the other hand, a psychology that focuses on the study of the soul and the spirit. Two conceptions of reality, which do not cross and living parallel lives.

Where is the passion? A huge excess of essence would be to break down the perception and the form of reality. Even the life could be. The perspective theory or the theory of the soul would have validity, but in practice this is not so...

The theory of vibration does not value consciousness, but all in the mind is vitality that vibrates and that doesn't seem to be detectable...

Shape and perception are at another level in the psychology of the soul by comparing it to the laws of perspective. Need for a theory that unifies this dissonance.

The desire is explained by the prospect and the other three effects, interactions essential and communicative attraction are explained through the psychology of the soul.

Can be explained through consciousness effects?

In the communication, awareness is a mediator that interacts between several consciences, being more communicative attraction much more dialogue there is. The assimilation led to a high degree, produces the sensation of imperceptibility of communicative attraction and essential interaction, since joining in an attraction priori. This attraction priori join also the essential interaction, creating a colossal effect, a super effect.

Is it possible to have a conscience without essence?

Love is the generator of desire in the psychology of the soul.

After the moods is the vitality that vibrates. The vibration makes consciousness something unique in essence. The difference between conscience and desire is the vibration. The mind is a huge vibration constant, balancing the contrasts and the apparent absurdity that occurs between theories, the soul and the perspective. The experiment is impossible to prove it; it's just intuitive; as well as his rebuttal.

The mind has some fundamental characteristics and they are met at all times: the essence of appearances, effects of desire, and the communicative attraction, essential to a priori and a posteriori interactions. This is the mind in perfect balance. Any change, however small that was, would be the disappearance of the same.
(Madrid, 01.01.2015)

NEBULAE

(part 3)

ON PSYCHOLOGY OF RANDOM

The brain as a set of processing machines of information through random and not selective, or divine processes, attempts to resolve conflict to adaptation to the environment and this compression (domination).

Our natural attitudes are caused by a random process and non-selective. Both our instincts or concepts such as culture or rationalism are not born of any principle divine, nor orderly; but that these processes are "Ordered" a posteriori interpreting them and giving them a logical sense to include, meet and above all dominate the space surrounding us.

Cultural stereotypes we are not given, but is their own a society that creates them. These stereotypes are some individuals to sort them, and thus appear to be their creators, the result of such management is the moral or material benefit that society can get out, when she identified in the screening (reflex).

The tradition throughout history has gone from metaphysical principles to scientific principles, but these have been logical errors to have interpreted the effects as causes themselves.

A work represents an effect made by an artist, a tiny part of his being, but not all, nor his being it; because the effects are not everything.

The work is interpretable, but not because its creator, this is incomprehensible and incomprehensible. Vanity and human pride strive not to accept such limitation for the knowledge of the thing itself, of the first cause and creates concepts that revolve about this random, but which do not become the thing in Yes (utopian rationalism). We can Intuit, imagine it, but never cover it, because it lacks logical principles. The logic is our "original sin" and we are condemned to not knowing the universe through it in its entirety.

Learning (imitation) makes us create a culture and identify us with her through the experience.

Violence and competitiveness are not innate to man, even though the Apostles of Darwinian sect to defend it. If something permeates the human being it is cooperation. The background of the altruism is selfishness, because there is always a beneficiary in Exchange. Such a moral considered selfish acts physiologically as healthy. In all time, gratitude, love, loyalty, human feelings, have been caused by selfishness, claudicating before him and a certain harmony among equals.

We don't have a negative side, but incomprehensible aside we interpret it as negative,
Natural changes are caused by random, unrecognizable acts.

The adaptation to the environment in which we live only proves that there is a movement, something that works, but not a selection. This interaction occurs genetically in recognition of the environment initially, to act on it later.

With the human genome project and the cataloguing of about 30,000 genes, was interpreted that that number was insufficient for the species and that there should be something beyond. Would be the soul response or a new Christian-moral foray into the science, to appeal at all costs from their imaginary principles of nature and thus minimize the qualities of the brain and that there may be substantial differences between a few genes and others,? What would that number lacked importance and on the other hand if the physiological processes in the brain tissue? Do you perhaps already know the expression of genes? I doubt it.

We ourselves are all, but know it and so it has always been. We have not evolved, simply we have become over time in relation to the environment and the recognition this.

Current technology is a half denatured alcohol that science is useful to understand (seize) the nature and nothing shows a progress if we compare it with primitive men lived with Spears to dominate space. Mind is currently governed by both parameters as in human prehistory; we simply changed the decoration, being our much more obnoxious than our ancestors who lacked moralizing and were therefore more free. Human complexity is not measurable, or pesable, but not for that reason is to invent imaginary reasons with the single object rather than the search for truth, but the justification of old dogmas of faith arising from the theft and appropriation of the alien.

Genetics is a Virgin, innocent, that can get into Christian-moral spider's Web and be eaten without any compassion.
(20-12-2010 Madrid)

COMMANDMENTS AND FAITH

The priests would believe in a society in which were accepted as the only representatives of the faith and the commandments represent the matter of their own experiences. There is an art to so doing and believers also have one similar to consider suitable this idea, leaking at the bottom of all modesty. The priests, from the craft that occupy and considering them fit to play it, are less suitable to assess all faith to be judge and jury. Faith Christian and priestly has generated in believers bias consider the society qualified to understand Christianity, being either well versed for the office of theologian. Deftly the believe to know the object unknown and distant to our knowledge from radicalism based on imaginary objects. What science if it is more convenient to comment, rating, judging from the deepest ignorance? Scanned from a physiological perspective Christianity is a religion of immoral and despicable. So far, akin to the priests, religious intolerance and prejudice have in the commandments and faith, their only reality. It is logical that society has Christian faith, since this is handled in scientific matters; as well as the society, poor, you feel identified with the salvation of the soul, the love of neighbor or the equality of all before God.

A commandment implies something more that faith; is also the feeling that this faith carries an obligation to abide by it (submission), without doubts about any issue can arise. It is incomprehensible of all belief; because it is based without reflection. Love of neighbor, to be intolerant in everyday life...

It can be seen that the Christian commandments are only a dogma of faith with a high degree of unity in those who profess it.
(21-12-2010 Madrid)

THE CHILD OF LACAN

Peering on psychoanalytic topics I found a brief writing that has left me dumbfounded by the folly and stupidity that holds. The first sentence it took to digest it because it was like a rotten bone;

He said: "between love narcissistic his penis and incestuous love for her mother, the child chooses his penis". Truly supernatural must be such child; I guess it would be a childhood memory of the author, fortunately for him.

Go to this phrase. The author interprets some extraordinary qualities in the infant, of course: is narcissistic, difficult to understand in itself, because a child is primarily selfish and his world turns the attention of the environment, rather than enhancing its character and less still because of one member of s u body.

What is so peculiar penis, so a child pays you so much care? Perhaps growing away from other members and that you can be in some striking appearance; little more. A child care or more obsessed by his height to his penis, for example; it becomes obsessed by measuring all the time alone, comparing peer of his age in school, both in physical aspects (strength), as in psychic (intellectual skills); but Lacan child seems to be studying in a private room or in a locked

House in the room.

A child begins to recognize his body with the growth of the same; as well as the appearance of the hair. The child compares with other children, and that makes it visible spots on the everydayness; perhaps the child of Lacan was born in the jungle, but eventually, it would have also there a mirror to enhance their "narcissism"?

The child of Lacan "recognizes" great love, but in its most negative way possible (narcissistic and incestuous), and makes Intuit a counter-measures on the author rather than on the imaginary child.

Incest is a "apotheosis fantasy" that reminds me of the fireworks of some romantic works of the composer Berliotz and his famous fantastic Symphony; can as anything a child even imagine incest if sex at such a young age? How to confuse it all or perhaps, what sad childhood due suffer similar "illuminated" Psychology and as a poet, capture its drama in a work. I say drama and not comedy, because his work is considered and that is valued in our times, even if the lie is worth more than gold and traded with it.

Finally, feels that this child has notions of duality and already "knows" the Exchange and trade, because "you must" choose between one option or the other... Oh, no; and why not stay with the two then, as any child would sound from its optical selfish? Or discard the two and self-sacrifice, on the grounds already monster like age? No, the child of Lacan selects and chooses one, which gives reason to a whole huge theory and monument to stupidity. The process continues and Lacan creates four times (phases) in the child:

1 - "child idealizes that everyone has a penis. There is no difference between sexual organs (feminine or masculine) "." Returning to the earlier, hardly the child goes to "idealize" and even less something that does not know does. What makes a child, at least one that is not the monster of Lacan, is live, imitate, go to understanding your environment; although in a simple way and erroneous, because the innocence and lack of maturity intrinsic, in addition to selfishness which previously referred.

For children there are different sexual organs, in the same way that there are different ideologies in the political world, because he lives in innocence, because he is... a child, to which the "master" Lacan seems to have forgotten, throwing him into the abyss of human complexity to such a young age.

2 - self-erotic's practices of the child. Alert the child to the loss of its member if persists the touching, giving rise to the Super-ego".

At this point is presumably that Lacan speaks of itself, because I don't think that it's universal standard alert children from such practices, unless they are justified in that what it called "super - I", which must be the culmination or intuition of personality , the apotheosis with rolls of drums in the final scene of one minor Symphony.

Do you want to Lacan subtly refer to consciousness? But how to refer to it from the unconsciousness of his theory? There is a theory of the unconscious, so there is an unconscious applied to the theory, which seems to be one of its greatest exponents. That "super - I" has more divine shades that Narcissists, it is the child turned into a God. In the God of the unconsciousness that loves so narcissistic and longs for incest and all by a member. How much longing for children!

How much longing to virility! It seems that you are playing all of a potential pedophile, enveloped by an aura of melancholy!

3. - visual discovery of the female genital tract. The child discovers the lack of penis into the girl.

"It's small, but it will grow".

The child of Lacan might have sisters and shower or change clothes with them, because in other examples, how might such observation? Perhaps little shy, since it wished to incest with his mother and is now released to the contemplation and comparison of the genital organs of your entire environment...

What horror! A child should thus suffer a trauma of lifelong, although Lacan has elevated him to the altar. In addition, the child has another extraordinary quality: guess the future as "super - I" deified and you already know that "it will grow". Such be must live in a deep obsession that makes you fantasize about male and female organs at all hours. Lacan child will have little time for studies and common games.

It is perverted innocence, as far as possible vitality. A sort of "old green child"; that is clear from the "super - I" of Lacan.

4. - "when the child discovers that women give birth, he deduces that her mom has no penis.

Here comes the anxiety of castration. Conditions: Vision of the absence of the penis in the woman; hearing evocation of parental verbal threats (this threat is unconscious). End of the oedipal complex; where the child chooses save your penis at the expense of relinquishing her mother and paternal recognition." The child does not infer that the mother lacks penis when he knows as a woman giving birth; but that suggests that he came of it and not the seagulls!

What obsession with the penis; It is to think about disorders hopelessly at your fingertips! For more I terror "comes the castration anxiety," what, of the penis castration? Mr. Lacan assumes that the child knows also the castration, its effects and trauma; it becomes "psychologist", takes him to his field and batters it spreading their evil. The figure of the father can serve to represent an image of the author's childhood, possibly; because not all children have had the misfortune to suffer verbal threats as the child of Lacan.

When referring to "this threat is unconscious,"... is it not rather 'imaginary'? Because a child's unconscious is underdeveloped in comparison to puberty... or is more of a "fantasy" that can lead to future mental disorders?

Lacan Finally, in a display of self deception and wickedness, makes merge the child threatened by his father (authority) with the recognition of this (submission); Choose i.e., the only thing that hurts you, if we take as good "verbal threats", and "domestic" it. Suddenly, God became a child and submitted to the authority. All a display of

pyrotechnics for dreamers.
(12-02-2013 Madrid)

1. Fan - If you idolize someone, worry about find a defect, as insurance has it. Not discover it, take for granted that you are a fan.

2. Political purposes - Politicians you care to divide society; lest one day together, an end to them.

3. Common objectives - The Spanish left confused nation State, wanting to finish off first, when the harmful is the second.

4 Decadent - Politics is the art of creating problems where there should be.

5. Political cowardice - Political pacts are immoral; a cowardice that threatens democracy and favors the oligarch class.

6 Greatness and squalor - Lincoln was just with the vanquished after the war, as opposed to Franco, which extended his hatred against the vanquished of the Spanish civil war, until his death.

7 Constitutional paradoxes - The Spanish Constitution prohibits the imperative mandate towards the members; but, what is the emission of the vote of an elector, then; and the party-list system?

8. Feedback - If there were no separatism, political rabble would last two days. Feeds on hatred and social tension.

9 Irrational - Defend separatism and to be left-wing left is a paradox that only ignorance can justify.

10 Redundancies - Commonly, politicians appeal to the rule of law in his speeches, which implies that there may be a State without the right, which is very unlikely. Admittedly, this expression was born in the 19th century to distinguish it from the police state; but the latter also is rule of law to contain laws.

11 Monarchs and oligarchs--The State was founded as a company in the service of the wealthy classes, for not paying taxes and speed up the collection of the same classes, medium and low.

12 Hand - The social democracy's exaltation of the State; is it therefore that both degenerate in unison?

13. Modern cowardice - Courage is no longer having value with the technological advances in the military field.

14. Own enemy – The State is the enemy of himself, since the demise of the barbarians (the Huns); i.e., from its very beginning.

15. Solidarity barbarism - The migratory movements are cheap labor for the richest States. Imperial barbarism follows its course, although it is made up of solidarity.

16 Dispersion - The birth of the Constitution and the State of the autonomies has diminished the autonomy of the State. The Constitution established as defective.

17 Separatism - What so easily grows, it tends to decrease with greater ease if possible.

18. Adaptation to the environment - Monarchy and Church are perpetuated for centuries, thanks to an extraordinary capacity to adapt to public opinion, even though it contravenes their principles.

19 Vassals and traitors - The political class is discredited because it lives subordinate powers that does not emanate directly from the people.

20 State laws - To destroy a politician, a judge to arrange it.

21. Procrastination – Leave it all to the last minute is typical of lazy and faint-hearted rulers.

22. The liquidators - Modern social democracy represents fascists masquerading as Liberals. A simple contraption linguistic and apparent social struggle with the purpose of obtruding masses.

23 State against nation - The independence parties, as well as the more radical, are kept much of face the State; but they do so gladly against the nation.

24. Ignorance - The Spanish left, if anything even more the most extreme, not do enough for the "right to decide" (self-determination, actually) of some autonomous communities, when already own Marx made it clear that Nations such as Spain, France, United Kingdom, or

Portugal, they were out of that right to conquer its constituent unit before the French Revolution.

25 Power and power - Power is to state that the power to the nation.

26 Form and substance - (Power of one) dictatorship and oligarchy (power of several), being different in its form are identical in the background.

27 Appearances - Some democratic States are far from achieving the freedoms of others authoritarian.

28. Reasonable doubts - The separation of powers is required to make a consensus Constitution. From this point of view, it is understandable to doubt there is freedom in the world.

29 Collective freedoms - The constituent period is based on the collective freedom in formation, to the constituent factor to create a Constitution.

30 Sacrilege - The Spanish Constitution is the Catechism of the oligarchs. They have even created a day dedicated to her; something that
It does not occur in any country in the world.

31 Breaches - If the constitutions will be applied to the foot of the letter, the parliaments would be dissolved.

32. The nation and the King - Spain not conquered nor discovered America; but it was a possession of the Kings; therefore, as a nation, still does not exist.

33. Bloody festivals - Catalonia celebrated the national day, an event that commemorates a defeat. France celebrates the storming of the Bastille, a horrendous act. Spain celebrates the Día de la Hispanidad, a genocidal act. The human being seems to not having dates in the calendar not representing horrors, wars, and innocent blood.

34 Civilization and democracy - We can hardly dream of a democratic system, when we are vaguely civilized.

35 Impoverish the poor - The success of the economists is in debt to future generations of lifetime. The downside of this is that a town that exceeds in naivety and ignorance allows it is.

36. Economic paradoxes - A financial system based on debt, is like an army that only available boomerangs as a weapon.

37. Rights and duties of the reverse - Would only have rights those who violate legality and duties those who comply with it?

38 Essentially ideological and moral prejudices - Christian-moral prejudice of rights conservative, takes you to not be reported as such; because there is a very noticeable contradiction between religious morality and the law of the neoliberal capitalist jungle. On the other hand, the progress of left-wing, social democratic or Communist, lacks that prejudice and expresses its ideology without shame. It could be sectarian affirm that "when someone says that it is not right, or left, we already know that it is right", said the French philosopher Alain; but analyzing the sentence in depth, see behind it a very appropriate moral burden to understand the essence of ones and others.

39 Nation and powers - Neither Governments, nor justice, bras of the State, are at the height of what constitutes a nation. The roar of the people before injustice and mismanagement of frivolous beings that momentarily hold power, serves in practice so that they perform their functions pursuant to or for the start of a revolutionary process that throw such daring and shamelessness. Social alarm work miracles, there where the political cowardice is committed not to act.

40. Of heroes to vulgar and merchants - The independence movement, had their leaders to act in a way romantic and suicidal. It was an idea that deserved the bloodshed and death if necessary. The postmodern bourgeois independence of the 21st century is far from such acts of heroism, according to dark matters, economic interests, forcing the masses to carry out what they are not willing to do.

41 Right and freedom - The right is claimed as the absolute value of individual faculty, through the demonstration. Freedom is required as the absolute value of the collective, through the revolution.

42 Landscapes - A young soul searches incessantly new landscapes. An old soul, in a melancholy way, revives those who remember his childhood.

43. Priceless - There is enough in the world to buy the creativity of a true artist.

44 Synthetic visions - The physiognomy reveals more politicians to their ideals.

45 On the fly - The thoughts, are conquered, nor are inherited; But coming alone.

46. Rule of law - A Government that based its policy on the use of the law, is predestined to fail, if legitimacy does not go with their actions.

47 Right and freedom (II) - Your rights begin where just mine. You freedom begins on par with mine.

48. Bad education - Indoctrination produces voluntary servitude, choosing everything that hurts you.

49 Existence and definition - The Renaissance did not discover the idea of nation, as it already existed in ancient Sumeria; although residents recognize it.

50 PARS - There are no two things equal, two equal beings. Gender equality is conceivable as legal, but never as a material.

Enrique Sousa (Madrid, 19-11-2017)